Contents

Meet Our Writer

A. Okechukwu Ogbonnaya
Okechukwu Ogbonnaya is Associate Professor of Religious Education at United Theological Seminary in Ohio. Dr. Ogbonnaya received his PhD from the Claremont School of Theology. He has published *On Communitarian Divinity: An African Interpretation of the Trinity* and has published youth curriculum for The United Methodist Church. A native of Nigeria, Dr. Ogbonnaya is married and has four children.

Introduction

This study book is a part of a series called The Bible People. This book is among the first four books we are producing at this time. They are: Bible Disciples, Bible Prophets, Bible Women, and Bible Missionaries. Hopefully, other titles will follow under other groupings.

We are aware of the cases where one person can fit in more than one grouping. A person can be a disciple as well as a missionary. A person who is a woman can also be in the grouping of prophets. Nevertheless, we are highlighting one aspect of that person's ministry in this series. It may be surprising to some readers to find out that a particular person is put in a grouping they never thought he or she belonged to. Our attempt here is to see that person from a different angle and perspective than we have generally seen in the past. But then, some persons will be in their unique ministry.

Each book at present has seven sessions on seven (or more) persons. Obviously, this is not an exhaustive list but rather a selective list of Bible people in a given category. Some of them have a large body of information and the others have very little, but we will still be able to learn valuable traits of their ministry and the impact they had in their own time and world.

In a few cases, two persons are studied in the same session because they belonged together as husband and wife (Priscilla and Aquila) or mother-in-law and daughter-in-law (Naomi and Ruth) or sisters (Mary and Martha). They jointly witnessed or created situations that impacted the history of the community in which they lived. That history has become the history of our faith and their impact has affected us as followers of the Way which God has shown us in and through Jesus Christ, who is our Savior and Lord.

We believe that these studies of the Bible People will renew our faith, strengthen our resolve to become worthy sons and daughters of God, and transform us into lighthouses and torches to give hope to the lost, and light to those in darkness.

Statement of Purpose: The purpose of these studies is to help us learn from the lives and ministries of some of the people in the Bible who have made a significant impact on the community of their time and who have contributed toward God's design for a God-centered life for all people, including us.

QuickLead®

This QUICK information will help you effectively LEAD a session of *Bible People*, either in a class setting or for your personal study. On *Bible People* pages look for the following:

ICONS

Six icons show you at a glance what kind of activity you are asked to do, such as reflection, group discussion, or interaction. See page z for more specific information about the icons.

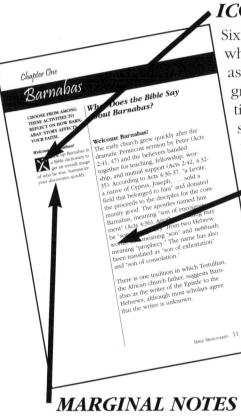

MAIN TEXT

The text contains the basic information about the Bible person or provides leads on where and how to discover more information on your own. You will also find open space there for writing notes from your research.

MARGINAL NOTES

Instructions for leading the session or for your own personal study are found in the margins. Questions for reflection or discussion are here too.

For more information, read the series introduction, and the other articles in this issue of *Bible People*.

Icons are picture/symbols that show you at a glance what you should do with different parts of the main text or learning options during a reflection or study session in the *Bible People* series. The six kinds of icons are

 Discussion—Either the main text or a marginal note will suggest discussion questions or discussion starters.

 Group Interaction—Either the main text or a marginal note will provide instructions for how to do a group activity that requires more interplay among group members than a discussion.

 Bible Study—Individuals studying *Bible People* are encouraged to dig into the Bible and mine the Scriptures to learn more about the Bible person and his or her contribution to the faith. Bible study may be done in a group or on your own.

 Bible Tools—*Bible People* uses the "discovery" method of teaching, using various Bible reference tools, such as dictionaries, commentaries, atlases, and concordances. Activities that require more than the Bible will be identified with this icon. (See pages 5-7 on "The Discovery Method" and the inside back cover for "Bible Reference Tools")

 Reflection—Group or individual *Bible People* students will have opportunities to think over questions, information, new insights, assumptions, and learnings. On occasion, the text will provide open space for written reflections.

 Worship—Sessions may begin or end with time for corporate or private devotions.

The Bible Discovery Method™ of Study

We are made in the image of God, and we yearn for God. Sometimes that is where our similarities end! As unique individuals in search of a relationship with the divine, we come to the task in ways as diverse as humankind. Each of us has a particular and personal perspective to the Scriptures because of our individual experiences. Our acquaintance with the Bible is influenced by our general attitude about what the Bible is and how it is to be used, as well as by a host of other factors. Each of us learns in our own way; some by doing, others by listening, others by watching, yet others by figuring out for themselves.

Discovering the Bible

There is no single "right" way to learn, although much published curricula and many Bible study teachers depend on a few tried methods, particularly lecture, reading from study books, and group discussion. While there is certainly value in these educational practices, a more interactive or personally invested approach often helps a lesson "stick" better. Persons remember best what they experience the most intimately.

The *Bible People* series study depends on what we are calling the "discovery" method. Rather than providing all the background information about a Bible person, we are inviting you as learners to do some of your own digging, through
- the Scriptures
- Bible commentaries
- Bible dictionaries
- Key word or topical concordances
- and other Bible references materials.

The items selected for further study can be found in most basic Bible resources. You do not need to have a specific dictionary or commentary. Most of these reference materials may be available in your church library.

Three Main Questions

The sessions are organized around three main questions:
- What does the Bible say about the person?
- What else would we like to know about the Bible person?
- How does what I know about the Bible person affect my life and faith?

Throughout the session you will discover what some or all of the references to each Bible person say and mean. Some information will be provided directly. Other information will come to you through your own discovery, perhaps by
- looking at maps;
- looking up key words in a concordance and then finding the appropriate passages;
- researching a specific Bible reference in a commentary;
- reading entries about key words, concepts, or persons in a Bible dictionary.

All of these activities can be done in a personal, self-study setting; most will also lend themselves to group work and discussion. The length of your study session can be adapted to the time you wish to spend in exploration.

Answering the Questions

In some cases, the biblical information is abundant. In others, the Scriptures may mention only a few verses about that Bible person. But whether the Bible offers a little insight or a lot, there is much more to learn. With hints and suggestions about where to look and what to look for, the discovery method draws you further into the life and times of each Bible person introduced in this series. To help focus the discovery method, the three organizing questions for each session provide a direction for investigation.

The first question, What does the Bible say about the person? delves into the Scripture text for specific references about the Bible figure.

Some of the persons featured in this series are characters whose record in Scripture is quite brief, perhaps only a few verses. Others are much more prominent. When the biblical information is scant, you will be able to review all the references. If the Bible figure is more prominent, only a selection of representative passages are indicated. If you want to dig deeper, the Bible reference tools will help you locate more information.

Whether the biblical references are few or numerous, the Bible and other sources offer much more information than you might immediately notice.

The second question, What else would we like to know about the Bible person? mines the less direct sources of information.

What is the context of the action? Who are the related characters who the featured Bible person influenced or was influenced by? What are the social and economic conditions that help us understand the person and his or her situation? Where does the action take place? These and other questions expand the picture and help you see more fully into the life and times of each biblical character in these studies.

Once the portrait has become more clear, the third question, How does what I know about this person affect my life and faith? helps you apply your new insights to your own life.

This question is the "so what?" or the "now what?" aspect of the study that links the ancient text to our contemporary lives and issues. In answering this question, the study facilitates self-discovery and, we hope, spiritual growth and transformation.

Bible People and Study Skills

All learners have different levels of acquaintance with the Bible and of skills to study the Bible. This article presents a few pointers for how to approach *Bible People*, depending on the level of those skills. Refer to the list on the inside back cover for a description of each of the tools mentioned.

Beginning Skills

Use a study Bible
- Use a good study Bible with notes, cross-referencing, and maps. Buy a new one if you need to.
- Be sure that the text is a translation that is readable and understandable for you. *Bible People* uses the New Revised Standard Version as its primary translation.
- Take some time to learn how to "get around" in the Bible. Use the table of contents to find the books and to see what else is in there. Many Bibles have articles, charts, maps, and other information in addition to the biblical text.
- *Get Acquainted With The Bible* (Abingdon Press) is an excellent introductory resource to help you learn what is in the Bible and how to use it. (Call 1-800-672-1789 and order #140463.)

Look over a one-volume dictionary of the Bible.
- Check to see if it contains a table of contents and/or an index.
- Read any self-promotional material that will help you understand what is contained in the dictionary.
- Then thumb through it, randomly reading any entry that catches your eye.

Acquaint yourself with a Bible commentary, perhaps a one-volume commentary for starters.
- Choose three or four of your favorite Bible passages and look them up, noting what new insights come from an expanded view of the text.
- Peruse the table of contents to see what else is there and skim through the articles.

Intermediate Skills

Introduce yourself to the other study tools: concordance, atlas, other sources.

Pick a key word from one of your favorite texts and look it up in the concordance. Is the same text in more than one passage? How is that key term used elsewhere?

● Look up a concept, such as *hospitality* or *marriage* in a topical concordance. What are the citations? How are these entries different from an alphabetical concordance?

● Check for a table of contents or an index, or flip through the pages to see what else is contained in the concordance. Read the introduction, if there is one.

● Thumb through an atlas to see what kinds of maps, graphs, charts, and other information is there.

Look up the places mentioned from one of your favorite Bible stories. How far are they from each other? What is the terrain like? What would a traveler be likely to encounter on the route?

Check to see if key information is provided for particular cities (like Jerusalem) or for prominent geographical features (such as Mount Horeb). If this is not in the atlas, use a Bible dictionary as well.

Read the text, then ask questions of the text.

● Who is involved in this passage? Who do they represent?

● Who is not present? Who is not represented?

● What is going on?

Who is the audience? What are they like?

Who is involved with the central figure(s) of the text? What impact do the characters have on each other?

What is the context? What is the central message?

What did that message mean then? What relevance does it have now? now for you?

What is not happening?

● What emotions might have been felt by the figures presenting the story, text, or action? by the audience? now by you?

What do you notice about the story, after using several resources to gain more information, that you didn't know or notice before? What difference does that make to your faith and understanding now?

Advanced Skills

Dig deeper into the cultural aspects and other details.

- Use the Bible study tools to look into details that the text suggests or assumes its original readers would already understand, such as, What did it mean to be a slave or widow or head of household? What did neighboring religions do in the same situation or region? Where is the action taking place and what was the situation there? How much is something worth? How long did it take to get there and what method of travel would have been used? What was the social/economic/political climate historically?

Use biblical-era sources in addition to the Bible and standard reference tools.

- Certain biblical passages are mentioned also in the Apocrypha or the historical context is the same. Check them out. Many Bibles include the Apocrypha, which most Orthodox religious groups (such as Roman Catholics) and some Protestant denominations (such as Episcopalians) regard as part of the canonized (or "official") Scripture.
- Look for references, concepts, and historical events in church encyclopedias, dictionaries, or historical writings. You may need an excellent public library or a theological library to obtain these texts, although most good bookstores have some biblical-era references.

Cross-reference passages to see what is said about the same or similar situation elsewhere in the Bible.

- When an annotated Bible provides cross-references or notes that refer to other passages, look them up.
- Many passages, especially in the Gospels, are recorded more than once. Look up the same event in another biblical book to see how it differs or agrees with the other citation(s).
- Ask yourself the exploratory questions as you compare texts.
- Use a concordance to look for several instances of the same word, event, social situation, and so on in the Bible. Look up the various references to see how the Bible's treatment varies (or not) to get a composite picture or overview of an issue.

Chapter One

Barnabas

CHOOSE FROM AMONG THESE ACTIVITIES TO REFLECT ON HOW BARNABAS'S STORY AFFECTS YOUR FAITH.

Welcome Barnabas!

 Look up *Barnabas* in a Bible dictionary to get an overall image of who he was. Summarize your discoveries quickly.

What Does the Bible Say About Barnabas?

Welcome Barnabas!

The early church grew quickly after the dramatic Pentecost sermon by Peter (Acts 2:41, 47) and the believers banded together for teaching, fellowship, worship, and mutual support (Acts 2:42, 4:32-35). According to Acts 4:36-37, "a Levite, a native of Cyprus, Joseph, . . . sold a field that belonged to him" and donated the proceeds to the disciples for the community good. The apostles named him Barnabas, meaning "son of encouragement" (Acts 4:36). Another meaning may be "son of prophecy" from two Hebrew words: *bar*, meaning "son" and *nebhuah*, meaning "prophecy." The name has also been translated as "son of exhortation" and "son of consolation."

There is one tradition in which Tertullian, the African church father, suggests Barnabas as the writer of the Epistle to the Hebrews, although most scholars agree that the writer is unknown.

Using the map, plot the cities in which Barnabas was believed to live and work, including Cyprus, Perga, Pisidian, Antioch, Iconium, Lystra, Derbe, and Syria.

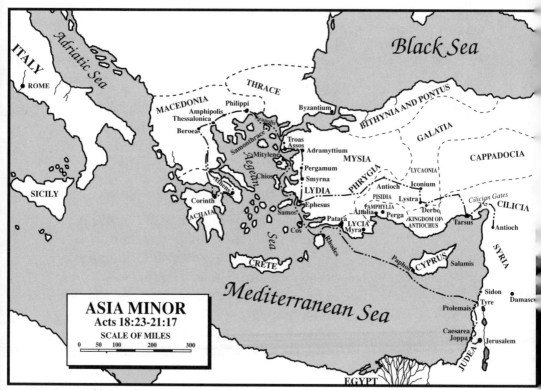

ASIA MINOR
Acts 18:23-21:17
SCALE OF MILES
0   50   100   200   300

From *Bible Teacher Kit,* Copyright © 1994 by Abingdon Press.

*Paint a Character
Portrait*

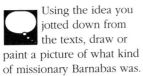 Using the idea you jotted down from the texts, draw or paint a picture of what kind of missionary Barnabas was.

Paint a Character Portrait

Jot ideas from the texts that tells you what kind of missionary Barnabas may have been.

◆ Acts 13:1-12

◆ Acts 13:42-52

◆ Acts 14:8-20

Research the passages and relationships of Barnabas with the persons mentioned in the texts.

- Barnabas seemed to be in the thick of things regularly. How would you describe the variety of his experiences?
- What does this tell you about Barnabas? about the potential in missionary activity?
- What were the natures of the disputes?
- How were they resolved?
- How might you have handled similar situations?
- How do you see the power of God at work in and through Barnabas and those situations?

Famous Relationships

Barnabas was an established apostle before Saul's (Paul) conversion experience. Saul had been an active persecutor of the early Christians. His reputation was widely known, and he was feared. Barnabas was instrumental in securing the converted Paul's acceptance among the faithful Christians (Acts 9:26-31).

The earliest church council mediated a dispute about disciples from the Jewish heritage. They insisted that Gentile converts come to Christianity by way of Jewish practice and law, such as by being circumcised. Barnabas was a powerful advocate for the Gentiles (Acts 15:1-35).

Barnabas had his share of arguments with Paul, including a disagreement about the participation of his cousin John Mark in a second missionary journey (Acts 15:36-41) and a fight between Paul and Peter over circumcision (Galatians 2:1-14).

What Else Would We Like to Know About Barnabas?

What's in a Name?

The act of naming and of having one's name known in the Bible has a significant impact. For example, God named the first man and woman, and the man named all the animals. This act of naming conferred a special knowledge and relationship upon the one named and between that one and God.

The apostles gave Barnabas a new name. His name was Joseph, which one would think was quite honorable in its own right, recalling the mighty son of Jacob and the earthly father of Jesus. Their purpose may have been to distinguish him from Joseph Barsabbas, one of the earliest followers of Jesus who was a candidate to replace Judas among the Twelve.

What's in a Name?

Check your concordance or Bible dictionary for the definition of both names (Joseph and Barnabas) and compare meanings.

- Why might Barnabas's original name have been changed?
- What do the names mean? Are there any differences between the two names?
- Do you know what your name means? Do you feel that God "knows your name," that is, has a special insight into who you are?
- If you could define your own name, how would you?

Who Were the Levites?

 Check a Bible dictionary for more information on the Levites.

Next look up the Scriptures and jot down some ideas about Levites. Check a Bible commentary to help you understand the passages.

● What implication would Barnabas's identification as a Levite have on his life? his missionary activity?

Who Were the Levites and What Was Their Duty?

Barnabas was a Levite from the island of Cyprus. Levites had particular legal and cultic (worship) responsibilities in the Jewish tradition. Once *Levite* was synonymous with *priest*. Through the centuries their role was separated from the priesthood and made subservient to it. Later the role of Levites, though still distinct from the priests, reclaimed most of its power and prestige in the community.

◆ Numbers 3:5-13, 40-51 (keepers of the Temple, consecrated for service; see also 8:5-26 and 18:21-32)

◆ Deuteronomy 18:1-8 (levitical offerings)

◆ 2 Chronicles 17:7-9 (teachers of the law)

◆ 2 Chronicles 19:8-11 (judges and mediators of the law)

Barnabas, an Encourager of the Poor and Needy

The Scriptures listed are just a few of the many passages that refer to the poor. Read the Scriptures provided and jot down your responses in the space provided.

- What do these passages tell us about the poor? about our responsibility for the poor?
- What effort did Barnabas make on behalf of the poor?
- What does Barnabas's example encourage you to do for the poor?

Barnabas, an Encourager of the Poor and Needy

Our first acquaintance with Barnabas is as a member of the early Christian community in Jerusalem where he exhibits a "big heart" (Acts 4:37) for the poor. What does the Bible say about the poor?

◆ Deuteronomy 15:1-11

◆ Luke 14:12-24

◆ James 2:1-7

Who Are the Poor in My Community?

Write down your information in the space provided. Start with the Bible references mentioned in the text. If you have time, use a concordance to look up other passages that refer to Barnabas's activity.

- Who takes care of the poor in your community?
- What does the Bible say about offering encouragement?
- What does the Bible say about dealing with new Christians?

Who Are the Poor and Needy in Your Community Today?

Barnabas introduced Saul, the new convert, to the Jerusalem church (Acts 9:26-30). Acts 11:19-26 reports that Barnabas was sent to Antioch to strengthen the young Christians. He displays his ability to encourage. He is described as "a good man, full of the Holy Spirit and of faith." How did Barnabas go about encouraging the new Christian in the passages? List ways:

1.

2.

3.

Commitment and Generosity

Ask class members to do a private inventory of the gifts and commitments they have given to their communities—family, school, neighborhood, and church. Have them use the following questions to get them started. Do not discuss the questions openly unless class members are willing.

- What have I given of myself, my time, my money, and my talents?
- Has this giving been from "leftovers"? Is it sacrificial?
- Could I live on what I give away?
- Is there anything I need to change?
- If so, how would I do that?

I Am Known

- How is Barnabas's example of one who encourages, consoles, and prophesies a model for you?
- In what ways can you do the same?
- Think about all the arenas in which you interact: family, work, community activities, and church functions. How do you model your faith?
- How does knowing that God knows your name encourage you?

How Does What I Know About Barnabas Affect My Life and Faith?

Commitment and Generosity

Our introduction to Barnabas shows him to be a generous man who sold a valuable piece of property to give the proceeds to the Christian community. Acts 4:32-37 models one expression of the early church: Christian communism—sharing all goods and redistributing them to each one according to need.

Somebody Knows My Name

While the name *Barnabas* and *Joseph* have special meanings, being known by God, regardless of one's name, is really the crucial issue. God knows you, and you are a unique and valuable member of the Christian community.

Your name does not have to mean "encourager" or "one who consoles" or "one who prophesies" in order for you to do those actions in the name of God.

Ask group members to think about a conflict that has been troublesome and unresolved. Then have them return to Acts 15 and analyze the dynamics of that situation—who did what; how it was done; the attitudes and assumptions that were challenged; the potential risks; the spirit in which persons engaged the controversy; the ways a decision was determined, supported, and carried out.

- What does this story suggest about dealing head-on with conflict?
- How is this resolution instructive for handling other conflicts?
- How might learnings from this example affect a conflict in your church, home, office, or elsewhere?
- How can your stance as a Christian help you take important risks? influence conflictive situations?
- Do you see this as a kind of missionary activity? Why or why not?

Worship

Summarize your learnings from the session and close with prayer.

You Can Do Hard Things

Barnabas seemed to participate in several activities that were controversial and others that were dangerous—clearing the way for Paul into the fellowship of believers, entering the fray concerning the circumcision of Gentiles, facing angry mobs during missionary journeys. He shows that there comes a time when true disciples must stand up for what they believe and take the risks associated with that stance.

Chapter Two

Jonah

CHOOSE FROM AMONG THESE ACTIVITIES TO REFLECT ON HOW JONAH'S STORY AFFECTS YOUR FAITH.

Meet Jonah and His World.

Ask class members to quickly call out what they know about Jonah's identity, character, and mission.

What Does the Bible Say About Jonah?

Meet Jonah the Prophet/Missionary

Jonah the prophet is identified as the son of Amittai. Second Kings 14:25 mentions his birth village as Gath-hepher in the territory given to the descendants of Zebulun, one of the twelve sons of Jacob. Scholars generally agree that the Jonah of the story may have only a tenuous connection to the historical Jonah, given the parable-like nature of the story that bears his name.

• Read Jonah 1:1-3. Jot down your information and feel free to interpret.

Using a map in your study Bible or from the Cokesbury's *Bible Teacher Kit*, find the cities of Gath-heper; Nineveh; Tarshish; and the territory of Zebulun.

- How far away from each other are they?

Short and Sweet?

Read 2 Kings 14:23-29 and information about Jeroboam in a Bible dictionary.

- What is said about Jeroboam? about Israel in general?
- Was Jeroboam the kind of king a prophet would be eager to support? Why or why not?

Research the relationship of Israel with Assyria.

- What was it like?
- Why would Jonah be willing (or not) to go there?
- What was Jonah's message?
- Why might he have been unwilling to preach to the Ninevites?

Short and (Not So) Sweet

Jonah prophesied during the reign of Jeroboam II, around 786-746 B.C.. Jonah is mentioned in connection with him in 2 Kings 14:23-29. Jonah's prophesy, unlike other prophets, was to a foreign nation: the Ninevites of Assyria. His message was short and to the point; a terse directive to people the Jews loved to hate.

Get a Broad View

Have the participants read through the Book of Jonah once. Assign chapters or verses to members of the group as your numbers will permit. Jot down notes in the main text.

- What feelings and attitudes of Jonah can you identify? of the king of Nineveh?
- How do those attitudes differ?

The Broad Picture

The Book of Jonah tells a great story about a reluctant prophet who is actually dismayed when his message is heeded. Jonah does God's will, but he also exhibits many of the worst traits of humanity. What is your portrait of Jonah? of the king of Nineveh?

Jonah's First Call

Jot down God's action toward Jonah in one column and in the second column Jonah's response as it relates to God's first call to him to witness. Skim again through Jonah 1 and fill in information in the main text.

- What is your opinion so far of Jonah as a missionary?

Gleanings from Jonah's First Call

God called Jonah to go to the Ninevites with a special message. The first call is in Jonah 1.

God's action	Jonah's response
1. Calls Jonah	Jonah heads for Tarshish
2. _____	_____
_____	_____
3. _____	_____
_____	_____
4. _____	_____
_____	_____

Actions, Reactions, and Reasons

 Using the chart, read the selected passages and note the actions, reactions, and reasons why the key figures in each scene do what they do.

Look at Reactions to God's Action (Jonah 1:1-16)

● Read Jonah 1:1-5. What is the mariners' reaction? What is the reason?

● Read Jonah 1:6-8. What is the reaction? What is the reason?

● Read Jonah 1:9-11. What is the reaction? What is the reason?

● Read Jonah 1:12-16. What is the reaction? What is the reason?

● Read Jonah 1:5, 8, 12. What is Jonah's witness at sea? What are the reasons?

Jonah's Prayer

Read the prayer (Jonah 2:1-9) and write down your impression of Jonah through the prayer. Compare the Jonah you find in this prayer with the Jonah you find throughout the story. Discuss your impression with the group.

Jonah's Prayer (Jonah 2)

We are never told that Jonah prayed for strength for obedience, or for the people of Nineveh, or even to be sure that the voice he was hearing was that of God. However, Jonah prayed when he was in deep trouble in the belly of the large fish. Jonah's prayer seems sincere and desperate, ultimately giving himself over to God's total control.

The Second Call

- What is the sum of Jonah's message?
- To what extent does the king heed Jonah's message?
- What is Jonah's attitude in delivering his prophecy?

What Else Would We Like to Know About Jonah?

Jonah's Second Call and Nineveh's Answer (Jonah 3)

Once Jonah actually arrives, his mission goes quickly. The king's edict covers the entire kingdom, including the animals. (Picture the animals in sack cloth!) The Ninevites repent and change their ways, and God repents and stops the destruction originally intended for Nineveh; God does not destroy the city or the kingdom.

The Ninevites

 Check the feelings of Israelites and Ninevites to each other. Select one or more of the listed Scriptures and jot down descriptions of the relationship between the two nations. Use a Bible commentary to help understand the Scripture references.

● What is Jonah's attitude toward the Ninevites?

Who Are the Ninevites?

The relationship between the Israelites and the Assyrians was one of great enmity. Nineveh was the capital of Assyria. This story is set in the reign of Jeroboam, although it was probably written at least a century later, certainly after the conquest of the Northern Kingdom of Israel by Assyria (722-721 B.C.). The Assyrians exiled all of Israel's rulers and leading citizens. The Northern Kingdom disappeared.

The relationship of Israel to Assyria is mentioned several times in the Bible, including:

◆ Genesis 10:1, 6-14 (origin of the Ninevites)

◆ 2 Kings 17:1-23 (conquest of the Northern Kingdom of Israel)

◆ 2 Kings 18:1—19:7, 32-37 (Assyrian aggression in Judah)

◆ Isaiah 37:1-37 (defeat of Sennacherib)

◆ Nahum (selected verses; an oracle against the Assyrians)

Review Jonah 4. Invite two class members to reenact Jonah's behavior; one as the story is written and one as Jonah might look in contemporary circumstances.

- In a few words, how would you describe Jonah's behavior?
- What ironies in the story become obvious?
- Why, do you think, was Jonah so displeased to have succeeded?

Using a commentary, look at how God uses the creation and destruction of the bush to make a point with Jonah.
- What is that point?

Jonah Can't Stand Success (Jonah 4)

Jonah's response to God's mercy on the Ninevites is bitter. He whines about having had to go to them in the first place and about God's change of heart toward them. When Jonah went off to pout, God still had more in mind for this reluctant missionary.

By divine intervention, God both created and destroyed a bush that Jonah had used for his own comfort. Again Jonah complained to God, wishing in this and in the previous instance to die, so great was his misery.

How Does What I Know About Jonah Affect My Life and Faith?

Attitude Check

- What attitudes and assumptions can you identify?
- Who seemed the most concerned about what God wanted?
- What efforts were made to discern and do God's will and by whom?
- Which figures in the entire story act like adults?
- When have you been like the mariners? like the Ninevites? like Jonah?

Check Your Attitude

Numerous underlying attitudes or assumptions have a great deal to do with how the story unfolds and with what happens to each character. Identify for each character as many of these preconceptions as you can.

◆ Jonah

◆ Mariners

◆ King of Nineveh

◆ Ninevites

◆ God

Clarify Your Expectations

Jonah may have expected exactly what happened: that the Ninevites would repent. His actions seem to indicate that he hoped God would destroy them instead. Then, when God's will was accomplished, Jonah suggested that it would be better to die. Do you think he expected to?

Expectations

● How would you summarize Jonah's apparent hopes and expectations for his mission and afterward?
● What did Jonah expect God to do?
● What did God do?
● How did God respond to Jonah's attitude?
● What circumstances or experiences were behind Jonah's attitude, expectations, and responses?

Jonah's Example

Jonah is not necessarily the best example of a willing missionary. He, like most of the ancient Jews, had a reason to despise the people to whom he was sent. The world is still full of enemies. The sins of racism, bigotry, and prejudice produce plenty of bitterness between persons, communities, and nations, yet God continues to press us into service for and with each other. Most of us will never be called to go to a foreign country to declare God's word. More likely, we are called to be God's people right where we are.

Jonah's Example

Invite class members to think about who would be considered their enemies and about the faithfulness and courage needed to respond to God's call to minister to others (even those who are not enemies).
● Are there groups or persons with whom you would be reluctant to share God's message?
● How might you know that God was sending you to a place you did not want to go?

- What attitudes do you have when God sends you to others?
- What attitudes do you have when God sends you to do what you do not want to do?
- How can you overcome your own reluctance to doing God's will?
- Do you find yourself putting "things" before persons and even yourself before the will of God? List ways in which your priorities are in or out of sync with God's priorities.

Sent to Others

 Brainstorm a list of persons and groups in your community for whom God has special concern and whom God would not want to perish.
- Who needs to hear God's message in your community?
- How are you or your church community obeying God's call to take this message to them?
- What specific measures can you undertake to fulfill God's call?

Worship

Summarize the main learnings of the session and close with prayer.

Jonah was angry with God because he was sent and then later on because his mission was successful. Jonah's priority was misplaced from the beginning, but that becomes much more evident in the story of the bush. He did not ask or labor for the comfort of the vine, yet he complained bitterly when it was taken away.

Sent to Others

God's response to Jonah was, in effect, Why should you begrudge my goodness to others, especially when I have been good to you? In addition, God has a much broader concern for the salvation of peoples and creation, not just for one bush. The sea captain (1:6), the king (3:9), and God (3:10) are very much concerned that no one should perish.

Chapter Three

Timothy

CHOOSE FROM AMONG
THESE ACTIVITIES TO
REFLECT ON HOW TIMO-
THY'S STORY AFFECTS
YOUR FAITH.

Meet Timothy

 Look up *Timothy, Lois,* and *Eunice* in a Bible dictionary and in the listed Scriptures.

- What is the overall picture that emerges of Timothy and his character?
- What do you find about his family that helps you understand Timothy better?

Use a Bible atlas to locate Lystra.

What Does the Bible Say About Timothy?

Meet Timothy

Timothy was one of the best known of Paul's companions and coworkers and possibly one of Paul's converts (1 Timothy 1:2 and 2 Timothy 1:2). His mother Eunice and grandmother Lois were Jews, while his father was Greek (Acts 16:1-4). Timothy's home was Lystra, a city visited by Paul on his first missionary journey (Acts 14:6). What else does the Bible tell us about Timothy?

Look up the passages to see what advice Paul gave to Timothy or to others that affected Timothy's life. Use a commentary to enlarge the meaning of these verses.

● What kind of standards did Paul give to Timothy? In what ways are they suitable (or not) for today?
● How, do you think, did Paul influence Timothy's life and faith?
● Who has been a spiritual or vocational mentor to you? What effect has it had on your life?

Review the Life and Work of Timothy the Missionary

The Bible mentions several formative moments in Timothy's life and faith, particularly in words of Paul to him or about him. Look at a few examples of how Paul's influence may have had a profound effect on Timothy's ministry:

◆ 1 Timothy 4:6-16

◆ 1 Timothy 6:20-21

◆ 2 Timothy 1:5-7

◆ 2 Timothy 3:14-17

◆ 1 Corinthians 16:10-11

Paul's Co-worker

Look up *Timothy* in a concordance to discover the books in which Timothy is mentioned. Read the sample Scripture passages provided to get an idea of Timothy's work with Paul (recognizing that most of these references focus on Paul).

- What was going on in the churches or communities that Timothy visited with Paul?
- How might you have dealt with the issues or conflicts?
- In what ways do you see God working through persons with backgrounds similar to Timothy's within your church? your community?

Timothy the Missionary and Co-Worker With Paul

Timothy traveled extensively with or for Paul. He is mentioned as a beloved colleague in twelve of the New Testament books. The following passages are a sample of the activities in which Timothy was engaged with or for Paul.

- ◆ Acts 16:1-11

- ◆ Acts 18:1-11

- ◆ Acts 19:21-22

- ◆ 1 Corinthians 4:14-17

- ◆ 2 Corinthians 1:1, 15—2:4

- ◆ Philippians 2:19-24

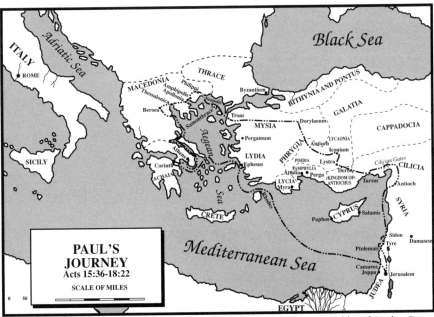

From *Bible Teacher Kit,* Copyright © 1994 by Abingdon Press.

Research the Bible passages to see what life was like in the early churches.

- What was Timothy dealing with?
- Have local churches changed much since then? If so, in what ways?
- How do you support your church leaders? How do you encourage those who disrupt the faith to refocus on the gospel?

The Price of Faith

Timothy's missionary activity was not without its price. Contentions and quarreling within the congregations could undermine the effectiveness of the gospel message. Dealing with these disagreements could be more than just "putting out a fire"; it could signal the dangers of persecution from outside the congregation or the negative influence of heretical notions within the church.

◆ 1 Timothy 1:3-11

◆ 2 Timothy 3:1-13

◆ 2 Timothy 4:1-8

Yet not all was difficult. Paul urged Timothy to guard against evils of various kinds, but also praised the work going on.

◆ 1 Timothy 2:1-4

◆ 1 Timothy 6:11-19

◆ 2 Timothy 1:8-14

What Else Would We Like to Know About Timothy?

Personal, Cultural, and Religious Issues

 Look up the word *Hellenist* in a Bible dictionary and the cross references provided to learn more about the influence of the Greek empire on the Jews and Christians of the first century.

● What differences do you discover between Greek and Judeo-Christian worship? culture?
● What did Timothy's biculturalism mean in the first century? (See Acts 16:1-5 and 21:17-26, for example.)
● What do you think of Paul's solution?
● What sensitivity did the early church show to persons from outside the Jewish culture?
● What do we do in the church today to understand and work with multiculturalism?

Have class members share stories of interfaith or cross-cultural experiences they know and how that situation affects their understanding of faith.

Personal, Cultural, Religious Issues

Timothy was bicultural and from an interfaith family. His mother and grandmother were Jewish Christians; his father was Greek. The relationship between Christians of Jewish culture and Greeks during this period could be difficult, even dangerous.

Christianity was under persecution from the Roman government, which had adapted many of the Greek customs (hellenization), and which worshiped numerous gods and mystery religions.

Multiculturalism

List the various interreligious or intercultural relationships within your church or community, such as the ones mentioned in the text.

● How are these persons regarded by your community? your church? you?
● How does the biblical message support or fail to support this regard?

Intercultural and Interfaith Families

Timothy was evidently held in high esteem by Paul (a "Pharisee of the Pharisees"), by congregations made up of predominantly Jewish Christians, and by churches with numerous Gentile converts. While being from an intercultural or interfaith family now is different from the experience of the early church, persons from these families may still face similar issues.

- How can you be a "missionary" to persons of a different religion or culture than your own?
- What would you have to learn to honor another culture or religion, while speaking on the merits of the gospel?
- How can persons such as Timothy contribute to our mission in today's global village where interethnic interaction is a political and religious given?

For example, some religious faiths do not allow intermarriage with persons of a different race or religion. This may affect the way children from interfaith and intercultural families are treated. Do you know how children from these relations are treated?

- White Americans/others

- African-Americans/others

- Hispanics/others

- Native Americans/others

- Asians/others

- Methodists/others

- Catholics/others

- Pentecostals/others

How Does What I Know About Timothy Affect My Life and Faith?

Faithful Mentors

Timothy had faithful mentors within his family (Eunice and Loise) and outside the family (Paul). The references mentioned earlier in the text reflect the affection and trust in which Timothy was held.

Can you remember those who were important for your faith formation? Jot down their names and what you remember about them that influenced your faith.

Faithful Mentors

Invite anyone who wishes to talk about the positive influence of the spiritual guides and mentors they have encountered. Urge group members to become mentors to others.

● What can we learn from Paul's interaction with Timothy for our ministry in today's world?

Discipleship

 Discuss with the group something they think could happen to one because of one's faith. Ask the members of the group to jot down the costs and benefits of their faith. Invite anyone who wishes to share them with the group.

● In what ways do you see God using you to minister to marginalized persons?
● To what new place might God be calling you now?

The Cost and Benefit of Discipleship

We know Paul was actively persecuted for his faith; no doubt his companions faced danger as well, yet they persisted.

● Jot down some prices you have had to pay for your faithfulness.

● Note the benefits of being faithful to your faith.

Worship

Summarize the main learnings of the session and close with prayer.

Chapter Four

Onesimus

CHOOSE FROM AMONG THESE ACTIVITIES TO REFLECT ON HOW ONESIMUS'S STORY AFFECTS YOUR FAITH.

Meet Onesimus

 Read through the text and the entire Book of Philemon to get a sense of the story.

Look up the main characters in a Bible dictionary to learn the "who's who": Paul, Philemon, Apphia, Archippus, and Onesimus.

The Rest of the Story

 Review the text and a commentary on Philemon.

- Where was Onesimus from?
- What does tradition suggest about him?
- How and when did he die?

Use the space in the text to jot down what we know or can assume from what Paul wrote to Philemon. Use the next space to imagine the other half of the story, based on the commentary and dictionary information you have seen so far.
Do this research individually

What Does the Bible Say About Onesimus?

Meet Onesimus

Onesimus was a slave, most likely a runaway, who belonged to Philemon. Paul wrote on Onesimus's behalf to the Christian Philemon to encourage Philemon to receive back Onesimus with love and mercy. Many commentators insist that the slave had robbed his master and had run away for fear of punishment.

The Rest of the Story

We know Paul's point of view and perhaps half of the story. We do not know the circumstances that led to Onesimus's "separation" from Philemon or what happened to Philemon when he returned. (Paul strongly implies that Onesimus will return, but we do not know that for a fact, either.)

- The course of events as described by Paul

or in small groups and compare with others what you have done.

Onesimus in the Bible

Look up the Colossians passage and the verses in Philemon and jot down notes in response to the question in the text.

● How would you characterize the relationship of Paul to Onesimus? of Onesimus to Paul?

Review the information about Onesimus from the commentary or Bible dictionary.

● What does tradition suggest about Onesimus and his life "after Philemon"?

● The possible course of events upon Onesimus's return

Onesimus in the Bible

There is only one mention of Onesimus apart from the Book of Philemon. Colossians 4:7-17 includes Paul's greetings from a number of faithful co-workers, including Onesimus (4:9).

How would you characterize the relationship of Paul to Onesimus?

◆ Philemon 10-12

◆ Colossians 4:9

What's in a Name?

Referring back to the Bible dictionary, research what Onesimus's name means.

Read Philemon 11 and the commentary on this chapter.

- What is Paul's point?
- How has Onesimus been useful?
- How might Onesimus be useful in the future?
- Based on your understanding of what church tradition suggests about Onesimus in later years, how has he been useful to the church?

Slavery

Review the text, then look up "slavery" in a concordance. Begin with passages from the Old Testament. Allow the questions in the text to guide you. (The Bible passages are suggestive not exhaustive.)

Then use a different tool such as a Bible encyclopedia or dictionary to learn more about slavery within the Hebrew system.

What's in a Name?

Paul uses a clever play on words (verse 11) to make his point about Onesimus and about what he hopes Philemon will do.

Useful is a typical term for good slaves; *Useless* was standard for bad slaves.

What Else Would We Like to Know About Onesimus?

Slavery

The modern conception of slavery often carries with it the connotation that the slave was ignorant or stupid or somehow inferior to his or her master. The slavery that was a part of United States history was involuntary (from the slave's point of view) and mindless of the culture or abilities of those persons forced to serve (from the master's point of view).

A biblical-era man or woman might fall into slavery in a number of ways: voluntarily, as in trust for a debt, for example; or involuntarily, as the spoil of war. There should be no automatic assumption (in any case, ancient or modern) that

Jot down ways in which the term *slavery* is used in the New Testament.

- What differences do you find in the usages of the word in the New Testament from the Old Testament?
- What differences do you see between slavery in the Hebrew system and what you know about the history of slavery in modern times?
- If Paul were asking Philemon to release a slave illegally, what do you think Philemon should have done?
- How does the Christian faith influence that decision?

the slave was not educated or "cultured." Slaves captured in antiquity, or in our own history, might easily have been from the upper levels of their vanquished society. We do not know Onesimus's social standing prior to his period of slavery.

Slaves were on the bottom rung of society and had no rights except those granted by the whim of their masters. In Paul's era, slaves could not be legally freed prior to age thirty. We do not know how old Onesimus was, but commentaries generally assume him to be a young man.

If release of Onesimus was illegal for Philemon, that adds a new twist to Paul's not-so-veiled request to Philemon that he not only free Onesimus, but that he send Onesimus back to him.

How were slaves acquired?
◆ Leviticus 25:44-46

◆ Exodus 21:1-7

◆ Exodus 22:1-3

◆ 2 Kings 4:1

◆ Numbers 31:7-18

How could a slave obtain freedom?

◆ Leviticus 25:47-55

◆ Exodus 21:1-7

◆ Exodus 21:26

◆ Deuteronomy 23:15-16

◆ 2 Kings 4:7

◆ Jeremiah 34:8-10

What were God's commands regarding the treatment of slaves in the Old Testament? Note that these laws were mainly directed to Hebrew slaves.

◆ Leviticus 25:46

◆ Job 31:13-15

◆ Jeremiah 34:11-12

Review the text and
respond to the
directions and ques-
tions in the text. Discuss
your answers.

Compare your thoughts to
Galatians 3:25-29.

Paul's Perception of Onesimus

Paul argues eloquently on Onesimus's
behalf.

- How many times does Paul refer to
  Onesimus as a slave?

- What are the various terms Paul uses to
  describe Onesimus?

- How does Paul encourage Philemon to
  look at Onesimus?

- What language does Paul use in reference to Onesimus and what does his
  admonition to Philemon about Onesimus do to the master/slave concept
  within Christianity?

Exploring Sentiments

 Skim the text and respond to the directions there.

Play a language game, either in pairs or in small, even-numbered groups. Using the adjectives Paul employed to describe Onesimus and Philemon (with some adjustments to be inclusive of both genders) ask participants or pairs within a small group to address their partners. After each adjective, have the group members describe the feeling or the personal emotional effect of the language used.

Exploring Sentiments

Looking at the Book of Philemon you will notice the language of relationships and you can infer the kinds of feelings they are meant to evoke. Keep in mind that Onesimus was a slave.

● The language referring to Philemon

● The kind of feeling you think this language may have evoked in Philemon

● Feelings this language used to refer to Onesimus may have evoked in the status quo of Roman society

How Does What I know About Onesimus Affect My Life and Faith?

The Missionary

Read the text and reflect on the hurdles you have or need to overcome before attaining your faithful goals.

- How might Onesimus's "rags to riches" story be like your own?
- What does this say to you about the power of faith and the influence of persons (like Paul) who are willing to ask in faith for what they want?

The Missionary

Paul's characterization in Colossians of Onesimus as a fellow traveler and "faithful and beloved brother" strongly suggests that Onesimus was freed and had became a strong leader and supporter of the early church. Onesimus is believed by tradition to have been a missionary who later became bishop, perhaps of Ephesus.

We do not know if Onesimus came from a humble beginning, but he certainly had to overcome his status as slave before attaining prominence in the early church.

- Hurdles I have overcome

- Hurdles I have yet to overcome

Your Point of View

Review the text and respond to the questions that follow here. Discuss your answers with one or two others.

- When have you needed or wished for someone to take notice of the "bigger picture" when your welfare was at stake?
- Who was there to advocate for you?
- How can you or have you advocated for someone else who was in a vulnerable position?

The Triple Bind

Review the text.

- When have you been caught between conflicting ideologies, beliefs, or practices that were each acceptable?
- If Philemon found himself in this bind, how might Onesimus have felt?
- When has your faith dictated a course of action that was either prohibited or not supported by your social boundaries or requirements?
- What did you do?

From Your Point of View

We know with some certainty Paul's place in Onesimus's life and can piece together some of the details that are not mentioned in the letter to Philemon. These few paragraphs remind us that there is always more to the story, any story, than immediately meets the eye.

A Triple Bind

Philemon may have been in a triple bind. Slavery was an accepted institution in his society, even for a Christian. The circulating Scriptures and spoken gospel messages were very clear about the requirements of loving one's neighbor and of kindness to all members of the household, including slaves, but slavery was not expressly prohibited. If Onesimus were under age thirty, which is not unlikely, considering the younger age of mortality then, he could not legally be released. Yet Paul was pressuring Philemon to let Onesimus go because it was the right thing to do as a Christian.

Oppression

Review the text and discuss the following questions.

- Who in your community would you identify as a modern Onesimus? Philemon?
- What is God doing through Paul for Onesimus, for Philemon, and for the society of slaveholders in this epistle?
- What vision of church community and responsibility do you see emerging in the Book of Philemon and in the example of Onesimus?
- What things can you learn from Onesimus's story that can help you in dealing with people like Onesimus in your community?

Worship

Review the highlights of the session and close with prayer.

Oppression

It must be remembered that slavery and other forms of oppression, no matter in what guise they exist or existed, are always unacceptable. Hence Paul's injunction to slaves must be understood as part of the progressive illumination of the human mind for the eradication of all such evil.

Chapter Five

Lydia

Who was Lydia?

Read the Scripture passages and jot down your findings in the space provided.

Take some time briefly to dramatize the interaction between this woman and Paul's entourage. Pay some attention specifically to her persuasion of them to accept her hospitality.

● Do you think that Paul and the other men would have been difficult to persuade if Lydia were a man?

What Does the Bible Say About Lydia?

Who Is Lydia?

Lydia was a woman from the city of Thyatira in the province of Lydia. Though the name *Lydia* may have been an indication of her native land, she was living in Philippi, a district well over one hundred miles away. What else does the Bible say about Lydia?

She was a business woman engaged in the trading of purple dye and cloth (Acts 16:14*b*).

She was one of the first converts of Paul on his detour to Macedonia (16:14*c*-15).

She offered her home as an act of hospitality to Paul and his company (16:15, 40).

Where Was Lydia?

Locate the region of Lydia on a map and look for the cities mentioned in the text.

Look up Revelation 2:18—3:13 to see what it says about three of these cities.

Where Was Lydia?

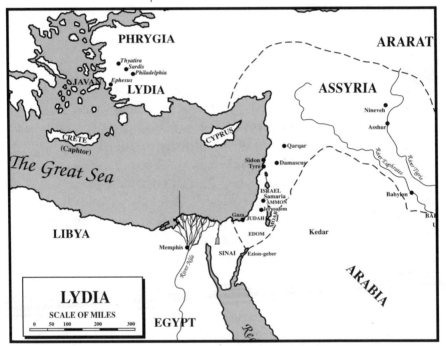

Adapted from *Bible Teacher Kit,* Copyright © 1994 by Abingdon Press.

The territory of Lydia borders the Aegean Sea in Asia Minor. Its major cities include Thyatira, Ephesus, Sardis, and Philadelphia. It is possible that Lydia took her name from this region.

We meet Lydia in Philippi, but she apparently came from Thyatira.

Lydia's Early Life

 Look up *Lydia* (the person) in a Bible dictionary or dictionary of church history.

● What else did you learn about Lydia?

Check a Bible dictionary to learn more about house churches. (Look up *house* first, to get an idea of the architecture, then look up *church* to get a better idea of the early worship gathering places.

● What do the passages in Acts tell you about Lydia and her household?

● What influence or relationship did she have with Paul and other travelers?

The Business Woman

 Look up *purple* in a Bible dictionary.

● What is *purple?*

● What is the significance of purple items?

● What is the general worth of purple?

● What does this imply for Lydia as a dealer in purple?

● Lydia is possibly unmarried and apparently wealthy. From what you know of women in that era, what does such evident independence suggest to you about Lydia?

Lydia's Early Life

Lydia was probably a devout convert (or sympathizer) to Judaism and then to Christianity. There was a church started at her house in Philippi where the Christians gathered to hear Paul. It is possible that as the first convert in Europe she was the leader of this house church.

Lydia, the Business Woman

As a business woman Lydia had opportunities to travel, buying and selling clothing. We know that it was through such business persons that the gospel was spread.

What Else Would We Like to Know About Lydia?

Jesus' Followers

Look up the Scripture references and write down notes about the women who were Lydia's female forebears in the faith.

● What did these women do?
● What were their social circumstances? their financial cirumstances?
● What difference does this make in your understanding of disciples and missionaries for the faith?

Jesus' Women Followers Set the Stage

Women were present from the beginning of the gospel. Check the following Scripture references and jot down the names of women mentioned as part of the Jesus caravan. Note their relationship to Jesus and, if mentioned, the kinds of ministerial activities in which were they engaged.

◆ Luke 8:1-3

◆Luke 7:36-50

◆ Matthew 27:55-61

◆ John 11:1-3, 17-37

Women in the Church

 Read the Bible passages about some of the women who were probably contemporaries of Lydia in other churches in other areas of missionary endeavor. Read also the text around these verses to identify the place these women lived.

● What role did they play?
● Who encouraged them in the faith?

 Check a map or Bible atlas and locate the cities where these women lived.

● If Lydia traveled throughout Asia Minor, might she have encountered any of these other women of the Christian faith?
● How close were they likely to have been?

Women in the Early Church

Women were very prominent from the moment of the church's birth. Note what the Scriptures say about the participation of women. Be careful to name the women where names are used.

◆ Acts 1:14

◆ Acts 9:36

◆ Acts 12:12

◆ Acts 21:8-9

◆ Roman 16:1-15

How Does What I know About Lydia Affect My Life and Faith?

A Worshiper of God

 Review Acts 16:11-15, 40 again to see what the Scripture suggests about Lydia's worship habits.

Check out this passage in a Bible commentary.

● What else do you learn about Lydia as a woman who worships?

Anwer the questions in the text for yourself. Jot down your reflections.

A Worshiper of God

First we know that Lydia was a worshiper of God, faithful and prayerful.

● What does it mean to you to be a worshiper of God?

● Do you have faith enough to hear when God is calling you to a new level of knowledge?

Lydia's Hospitality

In pairs, discuss the concept of hospitality as it is demonstrated in your church and in your own homes.

Discuss the questions in the text, using the space for personal notes. Share comments with the entire group if you wish.

Lydia's Hospitality

Generosity was also one of the principles we find in Lydia's life. She gave her time, her home, and her money to sustain the work of the gospel. The Scripture's use of the words *urged* and *prevailed* (Acts 16:15) may indicate that Paul and his companions were initially reluctant, even resistant, to accept her offer.

- In what ways is God calling you to be generous in, for, and through the gospel?

- How is your home a haven for the gospel or for supporters of the Christian faith?

- In Acts 15:40, Lydia's home seems to be the haven of choice. When have you persisted and prevailed in a matter of faith in the face of resistance?

- What were the rewards for your persistence?

Look at the questions in the text. Make notes of your own ideas and the results of discussion.

As a group, formulate at least a beginning of an action plan to investigate and meet the needs of disenfranchised women and families in your community. Include ideas about how to enlist the aid of women who are, like Lydia, able to give from their own means.

Lydia and Her Household

Lydia was evidently a strong woman, probably single or widowed, with a family and a prosperous business. However, conversion to Christianity might well have meant that she and her family were ostracized in their community, possibly in her work.

If Lydia were a single woman/mother, no matter how she became one, she would be outside the community's norms. But it was this woman who by God's blessing became the first European convert and primary supporter of Paul.

● List some categories of marginalized women in your community.

● How does your community look at disenfranchised persons, women in particular?

- While Lydia was well-to-do, not all women in her position were. What does your community do to reach poor women and to minister to them?

God in Your Life

Review the text and the questions. Write down notes to yourself about your own experiences.
- How can you be a missionary, either like Lydia or in your own unique way?

God in Your Life

If you are in a situation similar to that of Lydia's, where and how do you see God working through you?
- Where:

- How?

- Where:

- How?

- Where:

- How?

• If you do not see yourself as a person like Lydia, what in her life, faith, or experience might be a model for you?

• What does the life of Lydia mean for you in light of God's call to be a witness to the marginalized in society?

Worship

 Review the highlights of the session and close with prayer.

Chapter Six

Peter

CHOOSE FROM AMONG THESE ACTIVITIES TO REFLECT ON HOW PETER'S STORY AFFECTS YOUR FAITH.

Peter the Missionary

 Use a Bible dictionary to look for the different names used for Peter.

● What names did you find?

Look up those names in an alphabetic concordance to get an idea of how often Peter is mentioned.

In small groups or individually, read the Bible passages listed in the text.

● What does the Bible say about his background? Write notes in the space provided.

What Does the Bible Say About Peter?

Meet Peter the Missionary

Peter is referred to by several different names. We know he was one of the twelve apostles named by Jesus and later became the spokesperson for the group. Roman Catholics trace the lineage of the pope to Peter.

What does the Bible say about his background?

◆ John 1:35-42

◆ Mark 1:16-20

◆ Mark 1:29-31

◆ 1 Corinthians 9:5

Peter and Jesus

Form small groups and assign the passages for study. Use commentaries to help you understand the biblical texts. As you study look for consistency and inconsistency in Peter's discipleship.

- What happens in each of the passages?
- What is Peter's role in relation to Jesus? to the other believers?
- What do the ups and downs in Peter's life tell you about Peter? about the life of discipleship?

Ask the person or group studying Matthew 16:13-19 to check a Bible dictionary or commentary to learn more about Peter as the "rock."

- What does this characterization by Jesus mean?
- What does tradition suggest about Peter's future?

The Emergent Leader

Ask volunteers to read the passage, study it in a commentary, and to act out the election.

- How might these persons have felt?
- Was was the importance of restoring the number of apostles to twelve?

Peter and Jesus

Note that Peter's relationship with Jesus was not always smooth. Also note Jesus' consistency in loving Peter despite Peter's shortcomings.

◆ Matthew 16:13-20

◆ Matthew 17:1-8

◆ John 13:1-11

◆ Matthew 26:36-46

◆ Luke 22:31-34, 56-62

◆ John 20:1-10

◆ John 21:15-19

The Emergent Leader

After the death and resurrection of Jesus Christ, Peter takes a major leadership role with the disciples. Read Acts 1:12-26. What was this (perhaps) first "official" act of Peter?

Pentecost

Pentecost

Review Acts 2 to get an overview of that transformational event.

Use an atlas or maps to locate all the different nations represented in Jerusalem that day.

- How many nations were represented?
- How far away from Jerusalem were they?
- What native languages did these persons speak?
- How is it that foreigners understood what the disciples were saying?

Peter's Sacrifices

Note what Peter was doing that landed him in prison and how he was released.

Use a commentary or dictionary to look up *guard* or *jailer, prison, law, crime and punishment.*

- What were the responsibilities of guards or jailers?
- What was their potential punishment for failure?
- What were the prisons like?
- What punishments were inflicted?
- Peter's "crime" was preaching. What does his willingness to be jailed and punished for his witness tell you about him? about the faith? about your own responsibility to speak out about your faith?

The birthday of the church on Pentecost is one of the best known stories in the Bible (Acts 2). It is obviously a high point in the disciples's lives to receive the gift of the Holy Spirit. Peter plays a prominent role in that event.

Peter's Sacrifices

Peter's ministry was apparently never dull; sometimes it was dangerous. What extraordinary things happened to Peter?

◆ Acts 4:1-31

◆ Acts 5:17-42

◆ Acts 12:1-19

What Else Would We Like to Know About Peter?

Peter and Paul

Peter and Paul

 Peter and Paul are giants of the faith, but they did not always see eye to eye. Look up the Galatians passages and use a commentary to understand the content and context.

● How would you characterized their relationship?

Peter and Paul both served as missionaries to the Gentiles. (Peter's work will be covered in more detail later.) Paul mentions Peter in several of his letters and speaks about their interactions in these passages:

◆ Galatians 1:18-19

◆ Galatians 2:1-14

Peter, First Missionary to the Nations

Missionary to the Nations

Read this entire passage, then review Acts 3:1-10.

Using the map of Jerusalem, identify the gate (sometimes called the Gate of Nicanor) and the portico.

Draw a narrative picture of the Beautiful Gate and all the participants in the story. Establish the sequence of events that led to Peter and John's address.

● What happened?
● Discuss verse 6. What do you have that you can give in service to God?

Some of the texts you have examined already provide information about Peter's ministry to fellow Jews. Perhaps his first great recorded sermon is the one delivered on Pentecost (Acts 2:14-36). The second may be found in Acts 3:1-26, in connection with a dramatic healing.

Review Acts 3:11-26.

- What is the essence of Peter's message?
- What connections does Peter make between the need of the man at the gate and the gospel?

Ground plan of Herod's temple and courts, based on Vincent-Steve:

1. Holy of Holies
2. Holy place
3. Porch
4. Altar of burnt offering
5. Court of priests
6. Court of Israel (men's court)
7. Sanctuary gates
8. Nicanor gate(?) or Gate Beautiful
9. Nicanor gate

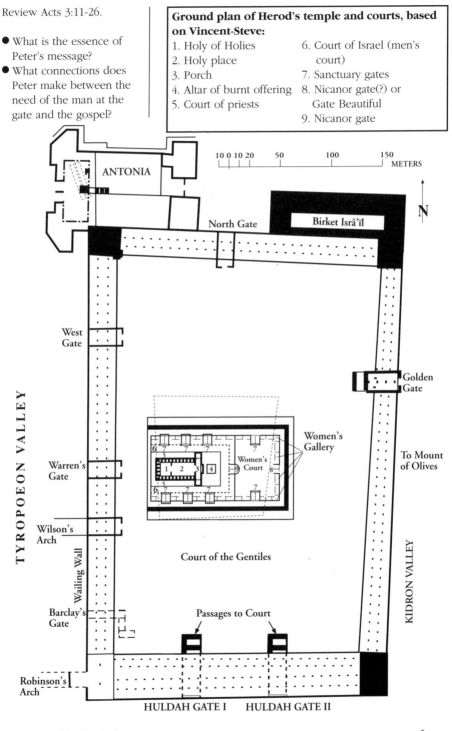

The Consequences

 Read Acts 4:1-12 and use the space in the text to respond to the first two questions.

● Who was there?
● How did Peter answer the rulers?
● Where did Peter locate the authority for this work?

 Acts 4:8 and 13 tell us that Peter was filled with the Holy Spirit and was bold. Use a Bible dictionary to get a better sense of what it means to be "filled with the Holy Spirit."

Look up passages dealing with being filled with the Holy Spirit in your concordance. Check to see if there is any connection made between being filled with the holy spirit and boldness in proclaiming God's message or doing some other form of work for God. Write down three to four of your findings in the space provided in the text.

Facing the Consequences

Peter and his companion John had been arrested for causing commotion by healing the man at the gate (Acts 4:1-31). Jot down the names and ranks of the persons who were gathered at the trial.

Write down the question asked by the leaders.

In the verse you probably noted that the main issue raised by the leaders was that of authority. The healing of the lame man was seen as undermining their authority. It is almost as though God could do nothing except with permission from them.

Peter's demeanor as revealed in this scriptural passage dealing with his interaction with the leader points out several things about Peter (4:8, 13).

Mission to Gentiles

Read Acts 10:1-48.
● What things did Cornelius do as preparation for receiving the gospel?
● What did God do to prepare Peter for ministry to the Gentiles?

Select members of the group to do a fishbowl exercise recreating Acts 10:1-43. One person will act for Peter, one for Cornelius, and others, if the class is large, for members of the household. The rest of the group will sit in a circle around them and observe in silence. After the fishbowl, invite the observers to answer these questions:

● What do you think is the significance of the fact that God used symbols within Peter's Hebrew background?
● What does Peter say about God? about Jesus? about the Holy Spirit?
● What does Peter say about himself and the other apostles? about the prophets?
● What was the result of this message to the Gentiles?
● What common threads can you find running through the messages of Peter to the Israelites, their leaders and the Gentiles in Acts 10?

Missionary to the Gentiles

Peter's ministry to the non-Jewish people was out of the ordinary for the early church. The apostles had concentrated on preaching to the people of Israel. It seems that they might have remained within their own group if God had not intervened in the lives of Peter and Cornelius (Acts 10:1-48).

If you want to find out more about the consequences of this action, read Acts 11:1-18 and 15:1-11.

Countless Adventures

Review the action verbs and make a list of the ways you have witnessed, viewed, fed, and so on.
- Is your list longer or shorter than you thought?
- In what ways is your life of faith similar to Peter's?

Answer the question in the text.

How Does What I Know About Peter Affect My Life and Faith?

Countless Adventures With Jesus

Peter was an ordinary man called to do extraordinary things. Look back at the adventures: announcing Jesus as Messiah, witnessing the Transfiguration, betraying Jesus and then being sent forth to "feed the sheep," viewing the empty tomb, seeing Jesus after the Resurrection. It may seem that your life could never be like that, but it can.

- How is your relationship with Jesus like Peter's? Feel free to discuss some of the "not-so-smooth" moments in this relationship and how Jesus redeems them.

Preparation and More

Privately or in small groups, review the spiritual practices that help you be in touch with God's will for your life.

Answer the questions in the text, and if you feel comfortable, discuss them with a partner.
- How can you give and receive support from your Christian community to be in significant ministry?

Preparation, Preaching, and Sacrifice

We have already seen that Peter was filled with the Holy Spirit. Note that Peter needed to pray for guidance.

- Are you filled with the Holy Spirit? What are some things in your life that convince you that you are filled or not filled with the Holy Spirit? For example, Peter moved from denial to accepting responsibility for proclaiming Christ.

Respond to the questions in the text.

Give prayerful thought to how you can deal even more graciously with the conflicts that inevitably arise in the Christian family.

Interactions With Others

Our relationship with God through Jesus Christ means that we have to relate to other Christians. Peter and Paul had their moments of friction.

● How do you deal with coworkers, friends, and fellow church members who need to be confronted?

● How do you deal with being confronted about a Christian cause?

Going to a New Place

 Respond to the questions in the text.

Consider working with others to remove barriers to break new ground for ministry. Covenant on how to support others and how to ask for support for yourself.

Going to a New Place

Peter was sent as a missionary to the Gentiles, a new and potentially dangerous place. He was arrested, even for preaching "at home," and had to justify his actions with the Gentiles to the Council in Jerusalem.

● What are "new frontiers" for you?

• What are the barriers you (or others) place that prevent you from going someplace new? How can they be overcome?

• What risks are you prepared to take for your faith? Who can support you?

Worship

 Summarize your learnings for the session and close with prayer.

Priscilla and Aquila

Meet Priscilla and Aquila

 Read the introduction and jot down notes on what you know about Priscilla and Aquila.

Skim a Bible dictionary to learn more about them.

What Does the Bible Say About Priscilla and Aquila?

Meet Priscilla and Aquila, Partners in Ministry

Priscilla (sometimes referred to as Prisca) and Aquila were Jews and natives of Pontus who lived in Rome during the first century.

What do you already know about Priscilla and Aquila?

Read the text and Acts 18:1-4 and note in the space provided the answers to the following questions.

Research this passage in a commentary.

Look up *tent, tentmaking,* or *leatherworking* in a Bible dictionary. Search also for information on Claudius.

Shared Circumstances

Paul sought out Priscilla and Aquila on his travels and stayed with them because they shared the same trade: tentmaking or leatherworking.

Another shared trait seems to be persecution. Priscilla and Aquila emigrated to the city where Paul met them because they could not remain where they had been.

◆ Acts 18:1-4

- Was leatherworking a lucrative trade?
- What kind of work did it entail?
- Where did Priscilla and Aquila live?
- Why did they leave?
- Where did they encounter Paul?
- What was their faith background?
- Who was Claudius and why did Aquila and Priscilla have to leave Rome?

Shared Journeys

Read the Scripture passages that tell where Priscilla and Aquila went with Paul.

Refer to the map to locate those cities or provinces (Pontus, Rome, Corinth, Syria, Ephesus).

Look up each city or province in a Bible dictionary to get an idea of the variety of experiences and cultures that Aquila and Priscilla encountered.

- What were those locations like?
- How far apart are they?
- What do you know about travel in those days? How long would it take to travel and what were the conditions?

Shared Journeys

Paul invited the couple to travel with him, and they did. The following passages provide clues to their journeys together.

- ◆ Acts 18:1-4

- ◆ Acts 18:18-29

- ◆ Romans 16:3-5

- ◆ 1 Corinthians 16:19

- ◆ 2 Timothy 4:19

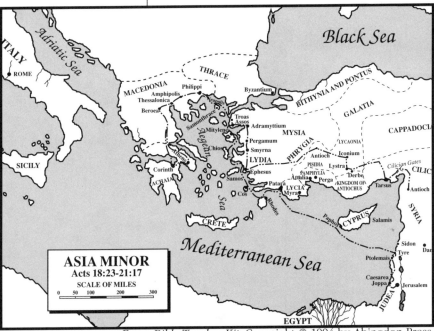

ASIA MINOR
Acts 18:23-21:17
SCALE OF MILES
0 50 100   200   300

From *Bible Teacher Kit*, Copyright © 1994 by Abingdon Press.

What Else Would We Like to Know About Priscilla and Aquila?

A Long Ministry

 Review the text.

Use a Bible commentary or dictionary to find the generally accepted range of dates for the writing of these three biblical letters.

● If you use the older dates for 1 Timothy, what does that suggest about the length of time Priscilla and Aquila ministered from the church in their home?

A Longstanding Ministry

Paul sends greetings through his letters from many friends and missionaries who have traveled with him or in whose house churches he enjoyed ministry and hospitality. In the passages mentioned in Romans, 1 Corinthians, and 2 Timothy, Paul extends greetings from Priscilla and Aquila and the church at their house.

Scholars are divided in their dating of many of the biblical writings, in part because the authorship of several letters is debatable. If the letters to Timothy are authentically from Paul, which many scholars doubt, they would have been written at about the same time as Romans and 1 Corinthians.

If the letters to Timothy were written pseudonymously by a colleague or student of Paul, it is likely that they circulated several decades later than the letters to Rome and Corinth. Should that be the case, Priscilla and Aquila may have had a long ministerial career.

Since we do not know the exact dating of those letters, and Scripture and tradition are silent on when the couple died, we can only speculate on the length of their lives and careers. It seems probable, though, that they dedicated their lives to the service of God.

Priscilla and Aquila Transmit the Faith

Some early church traditions have suggested Priscilla and Aquila may have written the Letter to the Hebrews, but most scholars disagree. There is no scriptural evidence that they wrote an epistle.

We do know that they taught the faith, since they had a church meeting in their home and traveled with Paul as missionaries. Acts 18:24-28 gives us a more personal glimpse into their relationship with Apollos.

Transmitting the Faith

Read the introduction to the Letter to the Hebrews concerning authorship of the letter.

● What does it say about Priscilla and Aquila?
● What are the reasons for suggesting them (or Priscilla) as the authors?
● What are the reasons against?

Read Acts 18:24-28 to discover something of their relationship with Apollos. Use a commentary to fill in details.

● How would you describe the relationship with Apollos?

If you have time, do some research on Apollos using a concordance and Bible dictionary.

● What else does the Bible say about him?
● What does tradition suggest about his career?
● How might Priscilla and Aquila have influenced his life?

Read the text and research the Scripture passages.

- What is your impression of the situation of the early church at that time?
- From these and other passages mentioned in the session, what are some specific ways in which Priscilla and Aquila were used in the ministration of the gospel?
- What do these and the other Scriptures tell you about their relationship to Jesus? to God? with the community?

Suffering for the Sake of the Gospel

We also know that the couple may have suffered because of their association with Paul and for their faith.

The atmosphere in which Priscilla and Aquila lived was hostile to the young Christian faith, yet they were not discouraged from being in ministry. Jot down your impressions about their situation.

◆ Romans 16:3-5

◆ Acts 18:12-17

How Does What I Know About Priscilla and Aquilla Affect My Life and Faith?

Partners With Paul

 Review the text and make notes in the space provided for the persons whom you know (specifically or generally) who need someone, such as you, to extend the offer of hospitality. Jot down the ways you can offer hospitality and the reasons and barriers that support or undermine the effort.

Discuss ways to overcome the barriers and to support others who need help or hospitality.

Develop an action plan to address this issue.

- If you were to travel to another city, do you think you would receive help or hospitality from someone in a church of your denomination, even though you would initially be strangers? Give a reason for your answer.

Partners With Paul

Paul apparently met Priscilla and Aquila on purpose and sought them out to stay with them, both because they were Christians and because the men shared the same trade.

Mutual hospitality was crucial in the early church because of the threat of persecution, the relative poverty of many missionaries, and the need for mutual social and religious support. Though our social system is different, the need to extend hospitality to the saints remains.

- Persons I know who need my hospitality

- Ways I can extend my hospitality to others

- Reasons for offering hospitality

- Barriers to offering hospitality

Review the text, then form small groups.

Ask each small group to talk for a few minutes about the courage and sense of purpose behind Priscilla and Aquila's movements, then about their own times when they felt God calling them to move on.

- What would it take for you to travel for the sake of spreading the gospel?
- On what occasion have you felt that God called you to move to a new place? Did you go?
- What barriers had to be overcome? What sense of purpose and courage was necessary to accomplish what you felt God called you to do?

On the Road Again

Whether by force or by design, the couple moved to several new places. Perhaps God's will was for them to spread the faith for a season and then to move on. So Priscilla and Aquila traveled throughout Asia Minor, at least until they settled in Ephesus. Evidently they had the independent means to travel, since Aquila's trade alone would probably not provide sufficient resources. They were forced out of Rome for their religious heritage and beliefs, so they moved on, meeting Paul and traveling with him for a while.

- Times for me to move on

Settling Down

Read the text and spend some time reflecting on the times and reasons why you feel God has asked you to stay put and work for the faith where you are.

- Priscilla and Aquilla used their vocation as a way to minister in the gospel. In what ways can you allow God to work through your work environment?
- Whether you travel or stay home, how do you see yourself as missionary for the gospel?

Faithful in Persecution

Read the texts and reflect on it.

- Priscilla and Aquila were teachers, leaders, and missionaries. What gifts do you bring to your community?
- What negative and positive reactions do others have to your Christian witness?
- How do those negative and positive reactions challenge your relationship with God? with others?
- What are some creative ways to meet those challenges?

Settling Down

The couple settled at least for several years in Ephesus. Paul's letters extend greetings from Priscilla and Aquila and the church in their house. Obviously when they located in Ephesus, they drew around them other believers and formed a worshiping congregation. Their stay there allowed them to provide the leadership necessary to build up this congregation.

- Times for me to stay put

Faithful in Persecution

Priscilla and Aquila were at risk because of their faith and, probably, because of their relationship to Paul. They also took aside Apollos, a bright man eagerly sharing the gospel, as far as he understood it. Acts 18:26 says they "explained the Way of God to him more accurately." Apollos might have resented that, but he evidently did not.

We do not always know how the message of faith will be received or what risks we assume by proclaiming the gospel.

Partnerships

 Discuss the meaning of partnership in mission. Develop a program for partnership with another group or with the General Board of Global Ministries. One way of making this process effective might be to expose your group to different persons or organizations who are involved in missions, especially if these persons help support their mission by working on another craft.

Worship

Review the highlights of the session and close with prayer

Faithful Partnerships

Can you think of other churches, organizations, or persons with whom you or the community needs to be in partnership for the sake of the proclamation of the gospel? How will you go about creating this partnership?

Formal partnerships can be established through the General Board of Global Ministries, 212-870-3660.